Sea Called Fruitfulness

To Mandy —
who knows the
cold —

all my love,

Sea Called Fruitfulness

Martha Carlson-Bradley

WordTech Editions

Martha Carlson-Bradley

xxx

Published by WordTech Editions
P.O. Box 541106
Cincinnati, OH 45254-1106

ISBN: 9781625490254
LCCN: 2013939308

Poetry Editor: Kevin Walzer
Business Editor: Lori Jareo

Visit us on the Web at www.wordtechweb.com.

Preface

The seventeenth-century Jesuit astronomers Giovanni Battista Riccioli and Francesco Maria Grimaldi were not the first nor the last scholars to map the Moon. But during a period when multiple, competing lunar maps were being produced, the Riccioli-Grimaldi map is the one that stuck. Many of its names for the Moon's features are still in use today, as is its approach to nomenclature: "sea" names (maria) for dark, flat regions, and astronomers' names for craters. No longer used are Riccioli's names for "lands" (terrae).

The map appears in Riccioli's *Almagestum Novum,* which was published in Bologna in 1651. Grimaldi is generally thought to have drawn the map from his multiple observations through a telescope, while Riccioli devised the nomenclature. The elder of the two friends by twenty years, Riccioli was better known in his own time than Grimaldi was, though Grimaldi is more likely to be recognized today, as the first person to discover the diffraction of light.

Acknowledgments

Specific sources for some of the phrases and events in the following poems and epigraphs can be found in the Notes section at the end of this book: "Camera Obscura," "Chrism," "Composition," "Diffracted," "Earthly Ambition," "Faithful Witness," "From its very internal nature," "Grimaldi, Erased," "A Life's Work," "Neither do people inhabit the moon," "Now and at the Hour," "Plea," "Sea of Moistures," "Vision," "Vocation," and "Without Quarrels."

I also gratefully acknowledge the following magazines for publishing earlier versions of several poems (many originally published with their first lines serving as titles):

> *Bellingham Review:* "Dead Reckoning," "Two Seas on the Moon." *Carolina Quarterly:* "Rare Earth Theory" (originally titled "Rare Earth"). *Diner:* "Aerial," "Allegiances," "Chrism," "Man in the Moon," "Plea," "The Red City," "That Night," "Vision," "Vocation," "Weltanschauung," "Wetland, Wasteland, Mire, Morass" (originally titled "Face of the Waters"). *Entelechy International:* "Metamorphosis" (originally titled "To Grimaldi, on Silkworms"). *Marlboro Review:* "Camera Obscura" (originally titled "Primavera"), "Composition," "Diffracted," "Heavenly Body," "Hypatia on the Moon," "Mare Crisium," "One Voice," "Orbita," "Riccioli in Old Age," "Scapes," "Scheme." *Sanctuary: The Magazine of the Massachusetts Audubon Society:* "Bloom."

I am very grateful for an Individual Artist Fellowship awarded by the New Hampshire State Council on the Arts, funded in part by the National Endowment for the Arts: this fellowship greatly assisted me in the completion of *Sea Called Fruitfulness*. My thanks also to the Poetry Club of New England for recognizing the poem "Man in the Moon" with the Gretchen Warren Award.

My sincere thanks to Martha Andrews Donovan for helping me obtain a copy of the dissertation of Alfredo de Oliveira Dinis, "The Cosmology of Giovanni Battista Riccioli (1598–1671)." I am also grateful to Audrey DeLong—not only for translating Riccioli's elogium for Grimaldi from the original Latin into English but also for giving me permission to use phrases from her translation in my poems—and to Alan Baragona for recommending her. My thanks also go to Peter Bradley and Jennifer Tousignant, for sharing their medical expertise, and to Grace Dane Mazur, for sharing her knowledge of silkworms. My deep gratitude goes also to the friends and colleagues who read or heard these poems at various stages.

I am very grateful as well to Lori Jareo and Kevin Walzer at WordTech, for helping my poems, once again, find their readers.

My sincere gratitude to the Linda Hall Library for giving me permission to use a detail from the Riccioli-Grimaldi map, from *Almagestum Novum,* on the cover of this book, and to Kristi Donahue for her cover design.

As always, I thank my husband, Mike Bradley, and our son, Sam Bradley, for their love and unfailing support.

Contents

III

I

Thy whole body shall be full of light.

—Matthew 6:22

Bearings

Suffusing graffiti, piazze,
alleys and avenues drenched,

the Moon is flooding too
the university's locked rooms—

every whiteboard swept with light—

as the Sea of Clouds above
forms a lifeless mouth.

Rain and Serenity fix in place
the right eye, the left.

And the two devout friends
who mapped these maria, men

untrackable now, unmappable,

must have walked in step
along streets called Paper and Failure,

crossing, preoccupied,
the Via of Chalks and Santa Lucia,

while Bologna's roofs and porticoes
cut the world into heated planes of red clay

and coverts of shadow—which blocked,
almost completely, any view of the sky.

Words on the Moon

to Riccioli

Among craters you named for famous men—
Aristotle, Ptolemy, Clavius, Kircher—
even Galileo, despite mistakes of faith,

finds his place. The human ideals
a rival mapped out, in kingdoms
christened Honor, Dignity, Justice,

you jettisoned. But since the Moon
whips up our weather, bending so close to Earth
the seas swell up to meet it,

you invented lands of Frost and Snow,
an inlet of Hot Days and the Island of Winds,
and waterways we never find at home—

your coves of Clouds and Rainbows
too rarefied to row on, science spun
into whimsy—as what is human seeps in

after all: the Bay of Epidemics heaves
off Peninsula Deliriorum. Delirium.

All that suffering
makes your Sea of Nectar, your Sea of Tranquility
depths to be longed for—sweet to the tongue
as well as the mind—like silk, no doubt,

on a weary swimmer's skin.

The Red City

to Grimaldi

As the Apennines arc, blue as a view of the sea,

across miles from skyline to camera
high in the tower—through centuries sprouting
hosts of homes, museums, shops—

the sight of your city rolls toward me
like heat: terra-cotta, ocher, rust, rose.
Even in photos, Bologna shimmers.

Paints took ages to grow this rich,
deeper pigments every year
disguising damage.

When you, a novice,

mused among buildings that stored
noontime sun, to release it
slowly by moonlight,

each pillar and wall you passed
warmed the air that touched you—
as you strolled along routes

of peach, pink, whole streets in the hues
of lips and palms.

Sway

Poor old Moon:
how much we've hung
on its hook in the sky:

crops and weddings, journeys,
jobs—we've launched them all
by the grace of its slim new crescent—

and when plans go awry, our work
slipshod, it's the waning gibbous phase
we've blamed for our failures. For us,

the Moon sports a human face.
Or a hare. Or an old man
with a dog and a bush.

And the frogs in April
keep making the usual pleas
in moonlight: small and slick

and cold, each body
vibrates with song.

Scheme

Pouring down from the Sea of Serenity,

waters that fill Tranquility feed, to the south,
bodies of Nectar and Fruitfulness.

What light in his daily reflections
did Riccioli assume he'd glimpsed?

From serenity flow all good things—? Or—
Tranquility comes to those who struggle against

the current, leaving far behind
nectar's musk?

The Moon may be tainted,
Aristotle claimed, too close

to Earth's corruption—what the Church
calls *sin,* venial, mortal.

Whether moonlight slipped into tangled sheets
or the Moon hid its face,

that snake of flesh, against Riccioli's will
as he slept, hot with his blood,

every single night reared up.

Earthly Ambition

Fingers cramped as they gripped
the quill, careers were made,

unmade. Letters passed
back and forth, Van Langren
complaining to colleagues,

The holy professor Riccioli
has altered all my work.

As the cleric wrote to Rome,
excusing himself, too sick to travel
in dog days of July—a mutt

writhing on fish guts in the market,
ecstatic, wild with oily riches,

rolled its body, belly up to the sky.

Sea of Fruitfulness

And all the while, on Earth,
the genuine sea, largely uncharted,
rises and ebbs and hides most of its life
where leagues crush down, their pressure
fatal to human lungs, and moonlight
never penetrates—though lanternfish gleam
day and night, over valleys dense
with tubeworms, undulant,
mountains on mountains looming,
too deep to climb: here,

and not on Riccioli's learnèd Moon,
spermatozoa flow, and blood.

The wind smells of salt.
Creation breathes.

Fertility, Mapped

In the show Riccioli makes of light
and shadow, waves of Fruitfulness

lap at the Land of Fertility,

synonyms bobbing
on the edge of nuance—

as grains of soil on Earth
warm in sunlight,

fragrance of humus released,

and plums by the treeful
grow plump. On the Moon

the brain alone is fecund,
the spirit fruitful,

and actual birth
is too messy to map.

Once, the belly of Mary

—who spoke with Gabriel, locking
his gaze with hers—

strained her skin
till it shone.

That Night

That night, as we reached in the dark
for each other again and the Moon
was new—so new it didn't show
one bit overhead, its round bulk

black as the sky when it rose
full speed from the east and the sperm
commenced its race toward the egg
in the unlit rooms of my body—

our son was just beginning
to begin—within hours

the Moon, still in flight,
revealing a narrow hint
of the light to come.

Wetland, Wasteland, Mire, Morass

to Riccioli

Neither earth nor sea,

your Marsh of Sleep brings only
blackout, stranded miles
southeast of the Lake of Dreams—

while your Swamp of Ice festers,
opaque as the Marsh of Decay. They brew
discomfort, odors. Disease.

Where I live, the blackbirds,
red-shouldered, dart among reeds
fringing shallow water. And every spring

our vernal pools refill;
tadpoles thrash in sacs of gel.

We're told that flesh must fail,
the soul fly off: a single road
to rebirth. But consider

the wafer, Giovanni, working
its miracle—body of Christ—on the hot

damp expanse of the tongue.

Dead Reckoning

To save the sailors here on Earth
this mapping the Moon began in earnest.

With features eclipsed precisely, minute by minute,
the Moon could give our globe its lines

of longitude; and ships could sail to port
with more than guesswork.

Abiding, the Sea of Showers and Sea of Clouds,
the Marsh of Fog, Ocean of Storms.

And Riccioli's terrae, missing from modern maps—
lands of Heat, Hail, Snows, Frost,

peninsulas named Thunder, Lightning—are trials
all mariners learn to navigate.

Even with black clouds bearing down,
thick and low—the sky is always

too high to touch—while the ocean, hiding shoals
as the crew sweats, is cold

and close. Its spray hits their faces.
It can swallow them whole.

Scapes

Is this a map of history—
Western thought on "the nature of man"
drawn as earth and water?

—or the mind of Riccioli alone

plotted out? The narrow Land of Manna
he tucked between Nectar and Fruitfulness,
all thirsts and hungers satisfied,

while his restless Sea of Humors,
fixed in the opposite hemisphere, endlessly
feeds the Bay of Epidemics,

where heat is oppressive, air
thick with stink.

The body as God's gift
meets the body of human decay.

And what map am I drafting?

Laid out for any traveler's eyes—
for yours—oceans of music, glittering,
surround whole continents daylight

seldom reaches.
                    How ornate the coastlines

eroding, accreting. Far out to sea,

in waves that are littered for miles,
fragments of paper floating and sinking,

little islands called Contentment
                                        drift.

Camera Obscura

Recalibrated, perfect,
a hole in the roof of the vault

let the Sun in miniature
descend from the ceiling—

to steadily trace the meridian
set in the floor. On the burning image,

for all to witness, sunspots
were shifting, left to right.

And the giant calendar counted down
to Easter: the first Sunday

after spring equinox,
the paschal moon, throughout

the wooded Apennines,

wild finches guard their nests
without instruction,

twigs and feathers
beading with mist.

Rapidly
small hearts beat.

Bloom

to Riccioli

I look up the Latin for moonflower,
Ipomoea alba—"pale worm"—
not sure if they grew in Bologna,

or if you'd notice them climbing the market wall
with their blossoms tightly furled at noon:
small rods like mops twisted dry.

Discreet, their habit:
they wait past sunset to flare
into fluted funnels,
                        wider, finally,

than your grown man's palm.

They're round and white as the Moon in full,
when their scent is a gift all night
to anyone, for any reason, still awake.

Love Poem, in Winter

From a sky that glows with overcast,
when the full of the Moon is flying unseen,

the snow is sifting down to gloss
cobblestone streets—and gathers,

past midnight, in bronze crevices
of Neptune, his curls and clavicles

black with patina. Snowbanks are growing
scalloped down empty porticoes,

flakes in college courtyards tumbling,
in numbers not infinite but still

too great to count: if cold,

they're not as cold as space, these stars
that land lightly, with a sound

softer than human kisses, repeated
as scholars, even asleep, keep piling up pages

that drift on every desk.

Lacus Mortis

How small, on this white world,
the Lake of Death is, northwest
of the Lake of Dreams.

No need, where no souls dwell,
to hold our multitudes:

it's mere memento mori
just off the Sea of Cold.

Rare Earth Theory

How much depends on chance—

the body glancing off Earth
just at the right angle, thrusting off

just enough matter to make the Moon, the Moon
just large enough, just the right distance away

to rule the tides and seasons, to let the first cells
ignite in a temperate sea.
      You know what happened next.

But gravity gives way to momentum.

And at last we'll lose that face
rising at twilight—

and its counterpull on Earth's axis—

and the way that tilt, steadied, alters the temperature
just enough to cue the wood-frogs to spawn
and gardeners to plant, generals crying

attack, retreat as dew fall mornings
spindles back into frost: all our time

a speck of snow
     catching the light

for an instant, falling,

just for the eye aligned just right,
by chance, to see.

II

From its very internal nature, the heaven has the capacity for generation and corruption.

—Giovanni Battista Riccioli

Plea

In his bargain with God
after calamity, Riccioli promised

all that first long night
to join the Jesuits, for life.

His bedding grew heavy,
hoarding blood and sweat.

Does a boy of sixteen
ever make vows he aches,
later on, to take back?

For hours his leg—

weeping serum, from hinge
of knee to articulate,
articulated ankle—

screamed for salvation.

Mare Crisium

The Sea of Crises doesn't lie
in the Land of Sterility—

it slaps the shore of Vigor, not far
from the sea called Fruitfulness.

I can make a case for that.

Leaving rumpled beds
soiled with blood from parted thighs,

how many poor souls, since Earth began,
have died in childbirth? *Saint Catherine,*

a rare female on Riccioli's map,

is found near Fruitfulness too, on the edge
of Nectar. But which Catherine is it—

the one from Alexandria,
steeped in books and astronomy,

or the saint from Siena: a virgin
women pray to, shaking, in throes of lust

and miscarriage? Tearful,
they've begged over centuries

for help. And the Moon indeed

is white, unbloodied.
And nothing dies

where no one conceives.

Two Seas on the Moon

Not just un-
complaining, *Serenity*

is *serenus—clear*
and *cloudless—*free

of any reason
to moan or mutter.

If a storm ever stirred
these depths, it's long past,

and no fresh tempest
threatens to form.

In Serenity's mirror
stars every night

find themselves gliding.
But southward,

where *Tranquility* promises
only *quiet,*

tropical air, unstoppable,
passes over

swells of water,
raising walls of fog

in silence—

though billows of weed
broken loose, mute,

well up to stain
the changing tide.

Heavenly Body

A crater blights the spot melanoma
marred my bicep—and lakes, basalt,
show where tubes once entered my body,
sucking the gallbladder out.

The appendectomy left a scar
and aftermath of stitches—small, pale flecks
like impact of asteroids—as mountains of varicose veins,
swollen, discolored, distort my right shin.

As for pregnancy, one, full term,

no stretch mark sullies that private flesh, belly and breasts
not as white as moonlight, not as cold,
but smoother than lunar landscape, their secrets
simply unrecorded. Not forgotten:

in that wave of hormonal blues,
in spite of joy, my child asleep beside me,

my body, abandoned,

was hollowed out—his soul no longer
my center of gravity.

Abundance

to Riccioli

In the hot summer air of your
Bologna—infused with fruit
and blossom, must and gutters—

plums in their delicate skins
were heaped next to stalls
piled with tripe and chicken eggs,
and flies, spontaneously everywhere,
wanted it all, dodging and landing
over and over, decay and sweetness
one and the same.

You took a vow at thirty
to stay forever celibate.
I married late.

Is it you, Giovanni,
who is pouring secrets
into bodies of water that never bear life?

Sea of Fruitfulness—Sea of Crises,
Lake of Dreams.

Silk Trader's Son

to Grimaldi

You were raised with bolts of gold
and crimson, emerald, cream—

where the faint odor of cloth
escaped the storage room,

silk, like wool, betraying through smell
how it springs from the bodies

of beasts. Tough cocoons
immersed in steaming vats

released those filaments
human fingers worked

on looms; and young men hoisted
heavy freight on the dock, their skin

shining with sweat.

Body is heft, and texture—
and your father read by touch

a fabric's value:

when he gathered brocade in his fist
—suddenly letting go—it made the sound
of its own falling weight.

Untested, fourteen, you left
at home your widowed mother.

As you took full vows,
a man of thirty-three,

the mantle's cool silk
laid on your shoulders,

did its scent bring him back—
however briefly—your dead,

your earthly father?

Diffracted

Broken—or bent—the light
fans out, little bands of color
fraying its edges: red, indigo.

And if this illumination
isn't pure, neither are shadows
cast in its center—as brightness and gloom,
Grimaldi noted, move by degrees,
penumbra to umbra.

At least on occasion, he wrote—
the Church would not agree—
light must undulate like ocean
to spill its banks like this, though
for proof, the beam has to pass
through a hole that's small indeed,
less than the eye of a needle,

the cone of brilliance created
most clear when dust
floats through the room

or smoke is set loose.

In extremis only
does sunlight reveal itself
this overtly, with darkness

not one thing or the other, in air
fragrant with fire, kindling like incense
giving up its ghost.

Breath

to Riccioli

When your mother bit down on the rag,
making her final effort coincide with pain
that squeezed at the top of her womb
before crushing down, her one thought

was to force you out—*now*—and only after
you slipped through her flesh and she let go
a groan of relief did she listen,
alert for your voice—

as air washed over your skin
like a tide, to fill your lungs
for the first time, and you cried out
your survival.

And though you never passed it on,

you shared that passage through blood and bone
with all of us, with Christ himself, and death too
would be like this: after hours of struggle,

at the end your insights were nothing, later,
you could breathe into words.

Metamorphosis

The silkworm, bite
by minuscule bite

in mulberry leaves,

swallows many times
its weight; and fibers

the larva fashions
to sheathe its body

keep out the world;

and the moth within
grows in privacy

predetermined wings
white as the Moon

and useless—

the abdomen bred
too big to fly.

Driven, the creature
never eats again:

clusters of eggs
blemish with promise
a green leaf

with a sheen like the silk
of priestly vestments

barely rustling

as the bride's full skirts
sigh up the aisle.

Hypatia on the Moon

Alexandria, AD 415

She whose name means *highest,*
most supreme, embraced the ideal

only: beauty of body, she said, was a rag
bloodied, washed and soiled again—

while beauty of mind was eternal as numbers
engraved in brass curves of the astrolabe

aligning Polaris, latitude, hour—

till time and the sky, dependable,
revealed her own position

on Earth: at the altar

her skin, perhaps
after her death, perhaps during,

was flayed for the sake of a pope—blood
splashing floor and walls
and candles and hands of the mob
crushed her eyes in their sockets,
shrieks of fury drowning
shrieks of pain—

though centuries since
Tranquility's coast is silent,

as the crater *Hypatia* waxes
every month, and every month

wanes.

Otherwise Always

The Moon in its flight
        covers so many miles

that anyone's view,
        though fixed in place,

will shift over time—
        with more of the western edge

revealed as it rises
        and more of the east

as it sets—this libration
        letting every eye

peek at the surface
        otherwise always

turning away.
        Like the near side

the far one
        waxes and wanes

in a perfectly synchronized dance:
        it lies in total shadow

while its alter ego, full,
        disturbs our sleep

with brilliance—the smallest flowers
clear as text on the quilt—

        and when no face above

shines for us
        the back displays itself,

white and complete
        to expanses of universe

empty of human life.
        All those hours

it seems that nothing but stars,
        fitful with distance,

riddle the sky—

        when bedsheets grow twisted
        and damp with sweat—

the far side is yielding
        cool, predictable light.

Passage, 1651

On a ship under way by grace
of Massachusetts slave laws,

the wavering beam of light

that stretched—a road on water—
back to the Gold Coast

was not admired by those
who were chained below deck—

whose pain could not be made
any more complete, by irony

or the Moon's blind face

or the beautiful names
that sages placed there.

Vocation

to Grimaldi

Were you alone the night you charted
the Lake of Death? Through the lens the Moon
stood on its head, mapmakers forced to draft

upside down. Dreaming, waking, pondering
Riccioli's thesis—you imagined the Moon always flipped:
no longer a face growing small in the sky.

Like you, Riccioli was ailing. My books
don't say how—fever? cramp?—or if you
suffered identical pain.

The Sea of Crises, completely landlocked,
is an almost perfect oval, beyond the Marsh of Sleep.

And the lunar surface met your eye as light
traveling in waves—a motion you captured in shadow,
your discovery called *diffraction*.

Before seeing your own study published
you were dead,
                    the crater that bears your name

far to the west of the Moon, edged out slightly
by one that honors Riccioli.

As you rechecked the contours of Death,
the telescope grew warm where it pressed your skin.
Below—Bologna milky with moonlight—

whole families slept. And your fellow Jesuits,
well and ill, lay down in their separate beds.

Vision

What miasma—fog or smoke—
blows between lens and Moon?

How close, or far?

Ancient astronomers used to note
how campfires smoldered,

bivouacs on the Ocean of Storms.

And years after telescopes
proved Schröter wrong,

he drew craters like circles
of trees—manicured glades

in full leaf on lunar surface—

revealing how knowledge
makes it hard to see: we find

what we know already.
Or think we know.

To the south of the Moon
that pit with its blast of rays

a thousand miles long

can't anymore be anything
that strikes my fancy: *star
chrysanthemum—puckered
stem end of an orange—
nipple in the solar system's
mammogram—*

It carries always now
the tag Riccioli bestowed on it:

Tycho,

who was just another human
on a list of scholars—

luminous. Flawed.

Sea of Moistures

Mare Humorum holds them all: blood
and phlegm, the yellow bile and black—
which drops with downcast sighs
toward a seafloor plush

with feces—as the blood wriggles
in rising tides and ebbing, incessantly
seeking flesh in vain to rub
and rub, against and in;

and the yellow bile, angry not to burst
at once into flame, hisses and spits
at the phlegm—which dodges abuse
with not a word, being cold

and wet. The calmest, it's merely
undercurrent.

Riccioli, early on, was mostly *sanguine*,
turning as health declined with age
phlegmatic, choleric.

He crossed the censors, late in life.

And his back was whipped
every week, an act the old man
did himself. Contrite. Stinking,

disembodied,

a stew of human excess pounds the shore:
semen, vomit, snot, sweat, tears.

Allegiances

Strange, how the craters
Riccioli and *Grimaldi*

don't find their place with *Tycho*
in the Land of Fertility.

How much closer the Jesuits
both are, at least on their map,

to misbelievers plunged
deep in Terra Sterilitatis:

Aristarchus, Copernicus, Kepler
set adrift in the Ocean of Storms.

But see them drift—
rayed and luminous—

their brilliance as far, maybe,
as Riccioli could go

in reconciling faith and data,

as the math of heretics
shone in simplicity, every equation

clear-edged as the shadow

crossing smoothly
the Moon's pocked face.

Without Quarrels

to Grimaldi

For you, young enough
to be his son, Riccioli sat still,

trusting, nearly dozing
as you guided the chill of scissors

at the base of his neck,
around ears, across forehead,

tufts of hair floating down

to the *rasp* of blade on blade
squeezed shut.

And you touched, briefly—

you brushed from shoulders
what his scalp had made, cell

by cell—the way, unmapped
as the far side of your Moon,

your skin beneath clothing
spun out its silk.

Grimaldi, Erased

from Riccioli's elogium for Grimaldi

Summoned from visible light
to illumination,

he assigned himself
the measuring of time.

How much love I owe:
unconquerable.

After vows and ardent
fever, short headaches—

in no doubt—

he handed over his soul,
almost smiling.

Serenitatis

to Grimaldi

Moving away, with all its maria
and terrae, light and dark,

increasingly small—

the Moon will keep its face
turned toward Earth—

and the Sea of Serenity

will grow serene at last—and the Ocean of Storms
become nothing more than a plain of basalt
bright in black space

just as soon as we're dead,
every single one of us.

Arguments called to mind
by words like *Tycho, Copernicus, Ptolemy*
will end. Nameless again,

formations you mapped for hours,
your eyes and fingers working in concert,

will stay precisely in place.

Like the storyteller's chair
when the household sleeps,

the Moon will be emptied
of human weight: free.

III

Neither do people inhabit the moon,
nor do souls migrate there.

—Almagestum Novum

Lingua Franca

I never mastered Latin, can't fully imagine
the phrases that sprang to mind

as Riccioli brooded all day on the cosmos—

though I'd guess when he bit into bread at noon
he was tasting a word from the Mass—*hostia*—

while the beans remained Italian, *fagioli*
brown as earth in the bowl.

And lines from Virgil, Ovid, Aquinas
he must have recited quietly

as his eye fell by chance on a flower
climbing the seminary wall. Above,

even without his steady gaze,
plains on a Moon more wafer than bread

reflected, like seas, the blue of the sky.

Fruitfulness Reconsidered

Its light more pure,
more white than the dingy rock
reflecting it, the Sea of Fruitfulness

means choice, and choice
demands the hush of the Moon
with its miles of solitude,

till understanding blooms, it seems,
all at once: think of Christ
in his desert—or rapt astronomers

deep in their skies.
                              After three days,

when Mary found her child
disputing, at twelve, with grown men
in the Temple—lit in the gloom, his face

was still unbearded—she gasped,
as the infant she'd once held
and the man he would become

met in the cast of his eyes
and lips—her own features
echoed there and not

just hers—some insight

breaking through at first
on her arms, legs: prickling—

gooseflesh.

Now and at the Hour

to Grimaldi

Nine young Jesuits,
three times three,

one whole day
counted every second

to test Riccioli's pendulum—

at sixty swings per minute,
for eighty-seven thousand swings.

Was it you, Grimaldi, coughing,
who tallied how long it took

for weights of clay and paper
coated with chalk

to drop from the tower,
gaining speed as they fell?

Was it your hand, like fate,
that let them plummet?

Or was it you below
who shouted *stop!*

as clay stamped its shape
in the dust?

Riccioli in Old Age

The sun showing first
as penumbra that turned

Riccioli's chilly bedroom
from black to gray

woke, as his eyes
flickered open,

pain—

which draped like a shawl
from the nape of neck

to shoulders and down
the length of his spine,

to swing a fringe of twinges
at the wrist. Hands above head,

Riccioli had aimed the telescope
for hours, his head cocked
at its own upright angle,

and he felt that night
all day, as he flung a shutter wide
or raised a book,

reminding himself of work
he pursued for the glory of God.

His scapula ached
through each sign of the cross.

Man in the Moon

With the naked eye, just before dusk is best
for perusing the Moon. The Sea of Crises

off by itself—a beauty mark
that graces the left temple—

is easy to locate. The Sea of Cold,
though faint, stretches to meet the lakes

called Death and Dreams: they form, in a row,
a long, single eyebrow.

As the softest shadows reveal themselves,
darkness on this face is not

one thing, but various tones
—till night sets in, truly black,

and the Moon starts to glow in contrast,
hiding its finer details in light,

when we notice mainly its mournful stare,
the mouth ajar, dismayed.

At the lowest rung of heaven
the Moon is looking the wrong way,

toward the blindfolded man who feels, hot and moist
on bare thighs, bare belly and scrotum,

the German shepherd's barked-out breath.

Again, the dog is growling, 1940, 2004,
while the Moon reminds us, in vain as it rises,

how every place is one place under the sky.

The Moon, Revised

Mary alone deposed the old order—
Diana, Artemis, Luna, Selene—

though not on the Moon itself,
except as a crescent to stand on, escalator,

as the Virgin ascends in paintings,
body and soul up to paradise.

For the Lord thy God
is a jealous God.

On Riccioli's map, scholars alone
inhabit the Moon and then

in name only—

mostly men, who never declared
they steered it, lucent, through space.

Riccioli knew:

they claimed the Moon through fame,
their fingers stained with ink.

In Manuscript

to Riccioli

Adding pages to his
pages, words to his words,
where he ended, you began:

Grimaldi was modest, cheerful,
kind—unfeigned and firm,
a son of light.

Loops of his letters
could be no one else's, clear
as the curves of his dead mouth

smiling.

And you faced every editor's
challenge—balancing care
with due speed—to lead

his thoughts from brain
to hand, from quill to type to learning
bound, preserved, still

talked about. You served.

Orbita

to Grimaldi

As you shift, once more, the telescope,
to track, exactly, the path of the Moon—

its speed astounds you.

And its silence.

All that light, all that weight
of the Moon's splotched body

flies with no flapping of wings
or grinding of wheels:

the odd hum of the ball accelerating
down Galileo's inclined plane

does not sing out as the Moon
rolls around Earth, which, you insist,

never moves from its spot
in the heavens—dead center—

where God, if you're quiet enough
and still, can always find you.

A Life's Work

Ten sextants he stored up, and many quadrants, parallactic scales
to determine the distance of objects, three tubes, interlocking,
to capture the glow of heavenly spheres, and nine telescopes—
one from Naples and one, on loan from Cavalieri,
made by Galileo himself—and Riccioli's best

extended fifteen feet, as the sky displayed its bright array
of constellations, planets, the Sun with its spots like clouds
caught in trade winds, the Moon with its cratered face
brought so close to the eye that older maps
cried out for correction.

And the scales recorded how far his sight had traveled.
And colored bands on Jupiter flanked its equator—
and he found, with Grimaldi, a double star
before turning back to Earth, to measure its mountains
and plot its latitudes, proportion of landmass to ocean
reckoned, as tables of longitude piled up,

incomplete when Riccioli passed to wherever it is
souls migrate—beyond his telescope's power.

Weltanschauung

to Grimaldi

His book was discounted, you know,
Riccioli's. Almost at once

no one at all

questioned the Sun as the hub
the Earth wheels around.

The heavens—reborn as space,
expanding—we can't pin down

at a single, centered point.

But your map of the Moon with its maria
outlives his theories.

When a man first planted his foot there

I was young and bookish, wise
and foolish, gaping at TV:

he walked with a tank of trapped air
to breath on Tranquility.

And our home, a marbled blue,
rose over white horizon—

your own towered city lost
only to distance.

One Voice

The sun shall not smite thee by day,
nor the moon by night.—Psalm 121

I lift up mine eyes unto the hills
from whence cometh my help—

and they're small, compared with a sun
fated to burst apart someday,

its power cast off in waves of flame.

Flesh of children is burning,
and flesh of troops—

and in China, in Pennsylvania, coal mines
are spreading fire across acres

underground—while protesters, a few,
keep their vigils, the nearby traffic

stalled and fuming—and still
letters get mailed to the editor.

Before five in the morning, alone,
the first bird, in all sincerity

perplexed,

poses his question: he doesn't ask
why he asks—but waits—

and repeats himself.

Intrusive and musical,
his query has broken my sleep—

one voice

clear of the oncoming chaos
as the sky, already, is turning light.

Where Jesuits Mapped the Moon

Winter, too cold here,
gives way to rainy spring—

every summer ushering in
humid days, when only dawn

is cool enough to climb
the leaning Asinelli tower. By fall

the fog rolls in
low and damp and night

drops all at once:

streetlamps grow haloed,
the Moon veiled—

diffused and magnified—

its light a medium
to swim through, reflections

of reflection, Sun to Moon
to Earth and back.

Each droplet shines in air.

Of Bodies Chang'd to Various Forms

In terms of the flesh, if not
the will—in those years
Riccioli wrote his theories

he could still have fathered a child.

Many men, older than he was then,
have done so—if not with women
my age. Is this

the real curse of Eve?

The chance for childbearing
passed—our bodies curve in
on themselves, dowager's hump
like a sickle. No—

like the crescent Moon
holding its old self in its arms.

Desire

After decades of months,

each womb in labor
relentless as death—

when the bleeding stops
for good
          even our thickest bones

thin out: porous as chalk.

When I'm done rubbing flesh
may I rub against gravity.

May time scour me down.

Stroked for years, may I grow
like sea glass,
                translucent
and smooth.

Reflection

to Riccioli

The more I learn, the less
this map is mine.

Nectaris, Endymion can't deny
storms without end

plague a full quarter
of this place: they rage
in ink, indelible.

Let me see the Moon

as you did: neither a face
nor a faceless pearl,

its uneven surface, for you,
never proved the universe
imperfect.

Every sea and continent
reflects all that's earthly,

all that dazzles our vision—

our urge to multiply, fears of illness,
desire for serenity

(as the Moon at twilight rises, gold in a violet sky)

—those concerns, I'm sure you'd say,
must fall like meteors blazing out

till the spirit is pure enough,
lifting like smoke up to God.

I'm alone in wanting flesh, alive,
to embrace your soul—
and breath in lungs,

to hear your voice
close to my ear.

Forgive me.

Faithful Witness

The crater you named for yourself, Riccioli,
is small—and so far to the west

as the Moon waxes, it's last
month after month to appear.

Thou hast given all to me.
To Thee, O Lord, I return it.

Composition

It is not the full Moon, but is constructed
of many phases.—*Almagestum Novum*

Even the most accurate map
is filled with inaccuracies.

Grimaldi's, especially,
patches together many nights,

since the Moon when full
washes out in the center, where the Sun
throws its harshest rays—

and the first and last quarters blur
in narrow brilliance, libration
taking hours to reveal the outer margins.

So, on paper, the Moon took time
taking on a measured tone,
with every sea and crater outlined.

This was his skill, to chart a vision
no lens can capture at once—
not even the lens of the eye.

Not in gloom, not in glare
do we see best—and not
straight on.

Details accrue one by one
till what results, we hope, is whole
and clear—from Terra Vigoris there

on the eastern rim, to *Grimaldi*
in the west—though tonight
this namesake is lost overhead,

submerged in too much light.

Chrism

to Riccioli

Cataloged, rare, your map,

once the sun expands,
will vaporize: every line

of the Moon's topography

lost to an Earth
that's turned to ash.

Flame will erase
all names, all pages

in history's book
of ambition. Nights

you spent with Grimaldi,

the lamp in your room burning
past the rules imposed on you both—

and fingerprints he, your friend,

left on parchment, with oils
his living body made—

will leave no trace.

Aerial

to Grimaldi

Overhead, a mortal couldn't see
the candle, lit and snuffed by turns
where you labor once more
to catch the Moon's proportions—

as Bologna stretches out for miles, its streets
rayed like spokes from your tower.

Burning late for childbirth
and deathbed vigils, scattered lamps
release a glow—faint and golden—
out past the edges of rooftops;

tiles of terra-cotta
corrugate moonlight.

Alone, the watchman's torch
yields its small glittering.
And blue-white saucers balanced—
improbable, tilting—on garden walls

are flowers bathed in light:
they're bouncing back what the Moon itself
reflects. And that sunlight, rebounding,
grows weaker with time.

Flesh of petals grows cool—while you
remain fevered, adjusting the lens

while the Moon makes its usual course
up and away and another night passes, another day,
as if they will never stop.

Notes

These notes are not necessary to appreciate or understand *Sea Called Fruitfulness,* but they do acknowledge the sources for some of the language and events in particular poems and offer guidance to readers who wish to learn more about Giovanni Battista Riccioli, Francesco Maria Grimaldi, and their lunar map. The Riccioli-Grimaldi map was first published in Riccioli's *Almagestum Novum* (Bologna, 1651), which is accessible on *Biblioteca Digitale,* http://fermi.imss.fi.it, last accessed March 17, 2012. The plates of the map appear between pages 204 and 204b. *Almagestum Novum* actually contains two lunar maps, one with features named and one without names. The map can also be found in the digital collections of the Linda Hall Library, http://lhldigital.lindahall.org, last accessed April 26, 2012. The cover detail from the lunar map is used with permission of the Linda Hall Library.

I'm grateful to, and humbled by, many experts in the history of astronomy and the Society of Jesus. In particular, Ewen A. Whitaker, in his *Mapping and Naming the Moon: A History of Lunar Cartography and Nomenclature* (Cambridge: Cambridge University Press, 1999), offers an invaluable discussion of the organization and nomenclature of the Riccioli-Grimaldi map and provides both a reproduction of the map and an appendix with a complete listing of Riccioli's names for lunar features. Scott L. Montgomery, in his *The Moon and the Western Imagination* (Tucson: University of Arizona Press, 1999), reveals how both science and folklore influenced cartographers of the Moon. The biographical information and discussions of Church censorship in Alfredo de Oliveira Dinis, "The Cosmology of Giovanni Battista Riccioli (1598–1671)" (PhD dissertation, University of Cambridge, 1989), were also crucial to my understanding of Riccioli's life, work, and times. Another work by Dinis, "Giovanni Battista Riccioli and the Science of His Time," in *Jesuit Science and the Republic of Letters,* ed. Mordechai Feingold (Cambridge, Mass.: MIT Press, 2003), 195–224, gives a scholarly assessment of Riccioli's scientific methods and contributions, as well as challenging arguments that Riccioli was a secret Copernican. Also in *Jesuit Science and the Republic of Letters,* Edward Grant offers an overview of sixteenth- and seventeenth-century Jesuit theories of cosmology, including Riccioli's, in "The Partial Transformation of Medieval Cosmology by Jesuits in the Sixteenth and Seventeenth Centuries," 127–156.

The following notes for poems and epigraphs are listed in alphabetical order:

"Camera Obscura": J. L. Heilbrun discusses the camera obscura in the Cathedral of San Petronio, Bologna—and the contributions the Catholic Church made to the study of astronomy—in "The Sun in the Church," *Catholic Educator's Resource Center,* http://catholiceduca tion.org, accessed May 12, 2005. This article was adapted from Heilbrun's *The Sun in the Church: Cathedrals as Solar Observatories* (Cambridge, Mass.: Harvard University Press, 1999).

"Chrism": Michael John Gorman mentions Grimaldi and Riccioli's late hours together in "Scientific Counter-Revolution" (PhD thesis, European University Institute, 1998), chapter 4, at note 74, http://sts.stanford.edu, accessed January 27, 2006.

"Composition": The epigraph beginning "It is not the full Moon" appears on the lunar map with features unnamed in *Almagestum Novum,* as cited in Whitaker, *Mapping and Naming,* 61–62.

"Diffracted": Grimaldi's experiments with diffraction were published in his *Physico-mathesis de Lumine, Coloribus et Iride* (Bologna, 1665). A description of these experiments is available at *Scienzagiovane,* University of Bologna, http://www.scienzagiovane.unibo.it, which was last accessed July 21, 2012. The short italicized quotations in the poem have been adapted from this source.

"Earthly Ambition": The italicized passage is adapted from Michael Van Langren's letter to Pierre Gassendi, which is quoted in Whitaker, *Mapping and Naming,* 62. Gorman discusses the excuse of illness in Riccioli's correspondence with Church leaders, in "The Scientific Counter-Revolution," chapter 4, at note 72.

"Faithful Witness": The italicized last two lines of the poem are part of the prayer Suscipe, which appears in section 234 in *The Spiritual Exercises of St. Ignatius*, as translated, for example, by Louis J. Puhl, SJ, rev. ed. (Westminster, Md.: Newman Press, 1963), page 102.

"From its very internal nature," epigraph to section II: Riccioli, *Almagestum Novum*, as cited by Grant, "The Partial Transformation," 139.

"Grimaldi, Erased": In a kind of modified erasure poem, all of the language of "Grimaldi, Erased"—including the order of the phrasing—is taken from Audrey DeLong's unpublished English translation of Riccioli's elogium for Grimaldi. The language is used in this way with permission of the translator, as are other quotations from the elogium that appear in this book. The original Latin elogium appears on pages 551–552 of Grimaldi's posthumous *Physico-mathesis de Lumine*, available in digital form at *Biblioteca Digitale*, http://fermi.imss.fi.it, accessed May 16, 2005.

"In Manuscript": The phrases in italics are quoted (in compressed form) from Riccioli's description of Grimaldi in the elogium in *Physico-mathesis de Lumine*, as translated by DeLong.

"A Life's Work": Dinis lists and discusses Riccioli's numerous astronomical instruments in "Cosmology of Giovanni Battista Riccioli," 19–20, 34–35, 63.

"Neither do people inhabit the moon," epigraph to section III: The original Latin inscription appears on the lunar map with features named in *Almagestum Novum*, as cited in several sources (with slight variations in translation), including Whitaker, *Mapping and Naming*, 62.

"Now and at the Hour": Dinis discusses Riccioli and Grimaldi's experiments with falling bodies in "Cosmology of Giovanni Battista Riccioli," 182–185. A discussion of how nine Jesuits helped Riccioli test the accuracy of a pendulum appears in Joseph F. MacDonnell, SJ, "Partners and Rivals in the Scientific Revolution," http://www.faculty.fairfield.edu, accessed May 10, 2005.

"Plea": Dinis mentions the accident that led to Riccioli's promise to join the Society of Jesus, in "Cosmology of Giovanni Battista Riccioli," 6.

"Sea of Moistures": The italicized words describing Riccioli's temperament appeared in several reports made by Riccioli's superiors, as cited in Dinis, "Giovanni Battista Riccioli and the Science of His Time," 223, note 98. In this note, Dinis also discusses reports of Riccioli's failing health. On pages 57–58 of "Cosmology of Giovanni Battista Riccioli," Dinis discusses the penance (flagellation) that the Church imposed on Riccioli.

"Vision": In *Mapping and Naming,* Whitaker comments on Johann Hieronymus Schröter's lunar drawings, first published in 1791: "Schröter consistently gives the rims of craters the appearance of an overhead view of a ring of closely spaced trees, even though many of those craters display sharp rims as viewed in the telescope" (107).

"Without Quarrels": Gorman mentions Grimaldi's cutting of Riccioli's hair, in "Scientific Counter-Revolution," chapter 4, at note 74. The title of this poem comes from a passage in DeLong's translation of Riccioli's elogium: "Franciscus Maria Grimaldus lived among us without quarrels."

About the Author

Sea Called Fruitfulness is the fifth poetry collection published by Martha Carlson-Bradley. Her other titles include *Season We Can't Resist* (WordTech Editions, 2007) and three chapbooks by Adastra Press: *If I Take You Here* (2011), *Beast at the Hearth* (2005), and *Nest Full of Cries* (2000). Her poems have appeared in such magazines as *New England Review, Carolina Quarterly, Marlboro Review, Valparaiso Review,* and *Zone 3*. Her poetry has been supported by fellowships from the New Hampshire State Council on the Arts and the American Antiquarian Society and by a grant from the Saint Botolph Club Foundation.

CPSIA information can be obtained at www.ICGtesting.com
Printed in the USA
LVOW06s1411301213

367449LV00001B/139/P

9 781625 490254